The Best Of

Viz Comic
P.O.Bocks 1PT
Newcastle upon Tyne
NE 99 1PT

*A myriad of
misguided missives
and enlightening epistles
from Britain's most
luminescent letters page*

*With a generous
sprinkling of*

*Words of wisdom, wit,
bollocks and shit.*

Crown ... House of ... ... Limited

All rights reserved. ... part of this publication ... reproduced or transmitted in any
form or by any means, or stored in any form of ... retrieval or other personal, including
photocopy, recording ... ...
... it is to be inventor ... ...

Printed, bound and paper ...

... One, Britain by BPC, Aylesbury

LETTERBOX

The PAGE with a PUNCH that makes your nose bleed

From John O'Groats down to Lands End they're the letters to us that YOU do send

It's BRIGHT, it's BOLD, it sets the TREND
It's the letters page with a BIG BELL END

Drink
BEER
Smoke
TABS

ISBN 1 870870 883

It's the page that *B* won't go away

Published in Great Britain by
John Brown Publishing Limited,
The Boathouse, Crabtree Lane,
Fulham, London SW6 6LU.

First printing October 1996

Printed, bound and gagged
in Great Britain by BPC Paperbacks

BRITAIN'S
B-WRITE-EST
LETTERS PAGE

The Best Of

If you think of
something shit
write it down
and send us it

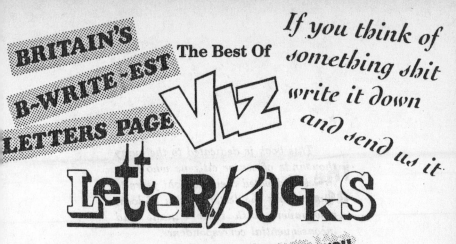

Viz

LetteRBocKs

The page that's not afraid to kick you
in the bollocks and then run away

The page that has ten pints and a curry, then shits its pants.

It's the page you
can bank on

to have

loads of

wank on

Edited by Chris Donald

Written by the readers
and the writers of Viz.
Viz is done by Chris Donald, Graham Dury,
Simon Thorp and Simon Donald.
And read by lots of people
whose names we don't
have immediately to hand.

Pictures drawed by Davey Jones.
Set on a computer by Sheila.
Spellings checked by Susan.

Britain's

HEART

WARMINGEST

letters page

This book is dedicated to the many thousands of senior citizens who have tirelessly devoted their twilight years to bombarding the letters pages of local newspapers with their inane and inconsequential correspondence.

And equally to the hard pressed newspaper staff whose unenviable task it has been to edit their senile ramblings down into one (and occasionally two) concise sentences.

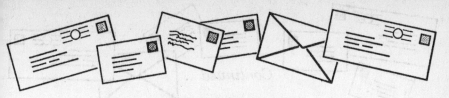

CONTENTS

Continued over...

Continued ...

Chapter One

≡ LETTERBOCKS

Imagine
My Surprise

IT'S going to be another one of those days, I thought to myself after running my wife over on the drive outside our home. But imagine my surprise when, looking through our old insurance policies, I realised not only would I be able to buy a new car with the insurance payment for my wife's death, but there would also be cash left over to buy a new telly.

> T. Cleaver
> Ashington

MY husband got a shock when he went to put on his newly washed shirt the other morning. It was covered in oat flakes, dried fruit, nuts and raisins. During my weekly shop I had mistakenly bought a large box of muesli instead of my normal brand of washing powder! Luckily we both saw the funny side.

> Mrs B. Murdoch
> Bedford

★★★

TOP TIP: At supermarket checkouts a Toblerone box makes a handy 'Next Customer Please' sign for dyslexic shoppers.

> **M. Axell, Middlesborough**

★★★

A FEW nights ago my wife and I were startled by a strange flashing light 200 feet above our heads. Only when my daughter reminded us that we lived in a lighthouse was the mystery solved.

> R. M. Coyle
> Sutherland

MY wife went to Amsterdam the other day, and I asked her to bring me back some 'hard core'. Imagine my disappointment when she staggered home clutching a sack of broken stones suitable for forming building foundations.

> J. C. Brighouse
> Nuneaton

IN a crowded supermarket car park my husband and I were unable to find our car. We felt proper fools when, after 3 hours, we remembered we don't have one. Luckily we both saw the funny side.

> Mrs E. Rolands
> Coventry

★★★

TOP TIP: Charities trying to raise money for a new hospice. Forget it. Build an opera house instead. That way the Lottery will pay for it. Once it's finished simply rip out the seats, and replace them with beds for the terminally ill.

> **S.L. House, Norwich**

★★★

WHILST watching an hilarious situation comedy, my wife, with tears of mirth in her eyes, mistakenly poured out two glasses of Paraquat instead of our usual beverage. Luckily we both saw the fungicide.

> Jon Sendel
> Sheffield

NOT long after we married my wife and I moved into a new house in Milton Keynes. Imagine our surprise to find our next door neighbours had a blue car - the very same colour as our own!

> Mrs B. Jones
> Milton Keynes

A FRIEND and I were delighted to spot a young lady sunbathing in the nude in a garden near ours. Unfortunately however, she was lying face down. We sat and watched her for over an hour, hoping that she would turn over, but she didn't. As you can imagine, neither of us saw the fanny side.

B. Harrison
Solihull

★★★

TOP TIP: Make your own Pot Noodles using a flower pot, sawdust and some old shoe laces. Pour in boiling water, stir, then allow to stand for two minutes before taking one mouthful, and throwing it away. Just like the real thing!

R. Tables, Jedburgh

★★★

THE other day my wife asked me to remove a scary beetle from the bathroom mat. Imagine my surprise when I discovered it wasn't an inch long insect with ten legs but George Harrison wearing a Frankenstein mask

Al Aska
St. Ives

★★★

TOP TIP: If you want to know the time during 'Baywatch' remember to put your wristwatch on the other hand.

P. Green, Wakefield

★★★

I TOLD my husband that I'd like a cheese plant for my birthday. Imagine my surprise when, on my last birthday, he handed me the deeds to a large dairy produce factory in Wales.

Mrs Godfrey
Weston super Mare

I PUT what I thought was insect powder down when ants invaded my home recently. But when our teenage son arrived home from college he was furious. I had spread £2,000 worth of cocaine all over our kitchen floor! He was even angrier when I rang the police and told them about the drugs. But I'm sure he'll have cooled off a little by the time they let him out of prison.

Mrs Gertie Pringle
Chipping Norton

★★★

TOP TIP: Prevent your milkman from becoming complacent by never ordering the same number of pints twice, and hiding your empties all around your front garden.

M. Cooper, Leyland

★★★

I ASKED my husband for a coconut plant for Christmas. I could hardly believe my eyes when he bought me a dessicated coconut treatment factory in the West Indies.

Mrs Godfrey
Weston super Mare

MY elderly mother is blind and over the years on each birthday I've given her a small piece of newspaper, telling her it was a £50 note. She has been saving these in a biscuit tin for years intending to go on holiday. Imagine my despair when she had a successful cataract operation recently and promptly cut me out of her will.

A. Lovick
Newmarket

★★★

TOP TIP: Caravan owners planning to use the A5 between Betwys-y-Coad and Llangollen on the first day of the Easter bank holiday next year , please stay at home. I'm visiting my girlfriend that day, and can't afford to be 7 hours late.

P. Bandwagon, Clywd

★★★

TALK about miserable neighbours. My neighbour and I share the same surname - Brown - which causes some confusion at times. In order to solve the problem I went round to see him the other evening and suggested he change his name to something more distinctive - like Titmouse or Sidebottom - only to have the door slammed in my face.

Mr B. Brown
Weymouth

THE other day it was our wedding anniversary and over breakfast I told my wife I loved her. "I love you too" I thought she said in reply.
It soon turned out that I had misheard her. The following day she packed her bags and left me to go and live with the pretentious Irish rock group 'U2'.

H. Chaparral
Luton

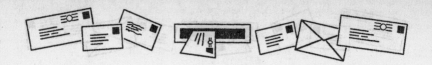

I TOLD my husband how much I'd like a rubber plant for the front room. I almost fell through the floor when he made me the managing director of a large tyre factory in Yorkshire.

Mrs Godfrey
Weston super Mare

★★★

TOP TIP: Get your girlfriend to suck a Sterident tablet whilst giving you a blow job. Not only will it give her a dazzling smile, your bell end will come out Bristol fashion.

J. T., Thropton

★★★

IMPRESSED by their TV advertising claim that they 'don't make cereals for anyone else' I purchased a packet of Kellogg's Cornflakes. Imagine my dismay when, two days later, I discovered my neighbour has a packet also.

Mrs I. Well
Wensleydale

★★★

TOP TIP: Olmypic athletes. Conceal the fact that you have taken performance enhancing drugs by simply running a little bit slower and letting someone else win.

A. Plasticman, London

★★★

I GOT a surprise last week when I plugged in our new lawn mower. It exploded, breaking almost every window in our street. "Hardly surprising", explained a fireman after extinguishing our blazing house. "It was a petrol mower."

P. Liddon
Peterborough

LAST Sunday after a bout of particularly passionate love-making, I lit up a cigarette for myself and my wife. Imagine my surprise, however, when I turned on the light and found myself in bed with our eldest son, Robert. I had come into the wrong room by mistake. My wife was waiting for me in the next bedroom!
Robert was most annoyed at the time as he is a keen athlete and he doesn't smoke!

Graham Nolan
Dublin

★★

TOP TIP: When speaking on the phone to someone in America, always start talking a couple of seconds before they finish their sentence. This will avoid pauses due to trans-Atlantic time delays.

D. G., Consett

★★

A FRIEND told me that the ornamental elephant on my sideboard should point towards the door and that it was bad luck to have it pointing towards the television. I laughed at the idea, but decided to turn it around as she had suggested. Ten minutes later I won the National Lottery.

Mrs K. Harrison
Surrey

★★

TOP TIP: Unemployed people. Why not brighten up Christmas by glueing glitter around the edges of your UB40.

Nobby Board, Wall

Chapter Two

★★

Are You Being Served?

I RECENTLY paid over £300 for a fridge which the salesman assured me had a light inside. How cheated I felt when I discovered that the light goes out as soon as you've shut the door.

P. Fox
Manchester

THE young shop assistant looked puzzled when I asked for the latest single by Shakin' Stevens.
Hardly surprising. I was in the butchers.

Mrs E. B. Harton
Luton

★★★

TOP TIP: Brigthen up dull bus journeys by sitting on the middle of the back seat and saying "Take her away, warp factor six Mr Driver", just before the bus pulls away from each bus stop.

Dominic Gartland, Consett

★★★

AT our local supermarket a loaf of uncut bread costs 34p - five pence cheaper than a sliced loaf. What they don't tell you is that it costs another £5.25 to buy a bread knife to cut the loaf with.

Mrs E. Forcett
Birkenhead

THINGS today aren't as well made as they used to be. I bought a mop in a good old fashioned hardware shop some 40 years ago and it's still as good as new. In all that time it has only required three new heads, and two new handles.

J. Aldbury
Oldham

★★

TOP TIP: Create a more relaxing atmosphere in your fridge by installing a dimmer switch.

Roger Radio, Faversham

★★

HOW ridiculous it is supermarkets selling fruit by the pound when apples are so much heavier than grapes.

Mrs Elsa Thompson
Bishopsgate

★★

TOP TIP: Hitch-hikers. Improve your chances of getting a lift by NOT dressing up as a hunt saboteur and waving half a cardboard box at passing motorists.

John Kean, London SE1

★★

AFTER buying a tin of 'Alphabetti Spaghetti' in my local supermarket I was horrified to find that by arranging the letters on the side of my young daughter's plate, not only was I able to spell the word 'fuck', but also 'shit' and 'wank' as well. It's coming to something when supermarkets openly peddle filth like this to young children.

Mrs J. Blackford
Eversham

WHAT a con these advertisements are. I have been smoking Dr Whites and Tampax for over ten years, and I still can't swim or play tennis.

> M. Majaffa
> Titchfield Common

THIS consumer terrorism has gone too far. First it was glass in pet food, then fuse wire in baby food. And now while eating my cornflakes this morning I almost choked on a small plastic dinosaur.

What will these callous people think of next?

> S. Jones
> York

★★★

TOP TIP: Ladies. Check both your breasts are the same size by making a plaster mould of each. Fill both moulds with water, then pour the contents into two separate measuring jugs. The amounts of water in each will tell you which 'jug' is the bigger.

> **Mr S. Brown, Peckham**

★★★

I THINK 'Lucozade' should be renamed 'Loo-cozade' because it tastes like piss.

> John de Pledge
> Solihull

IT'S no wonder these match manufacturers make such fat profits. I find that I only ever use half a match before blowing it out. For a moderate smoker like myself on 80 cigarettes a day, this works out at a loss of almost 25p a week on unused matches - that's a staggering £10 a year. It's almost enough to make you give up smoking.

> A. Sinclair
> Bristol

THE other day the supermarket check-out girl handed me a list of my shopping along with my change. Surely it would make more sense for them to hand housewives this list before we do our shopping thus saving us the bother of having to write a shopping list.

Mrs G. Stephens
Stevenage

★★★

TOP TIP: Tie a fish on a piece of string, climb up onto your neighbour's roof, and dangle the fish in front of his window. He'll think his house is underwater.

R.R., Kent

★★★

WHY is it that whenever you dial a wrong number, it is never engaged? Is it any wonder British Telecom's tills continue to ring up such massive profits at our expense?

B. Harrison
Solihull

AS it was Sunday and the post office was closed, I offered my neighbour, who is unemployed, 38p to deliver a letter to my sister in Devon (12p more than the going rate of 26p first class). However, he flatly refused. Is it any wonder that there are so many unemployed, when people like him are simply not interested in the idea of work.

Mr B. Evans,
Berwick on Tweed

★★

TOP TIP: A wire brush makes an ideal bed of nails for a hamster.

John Tait, Thropton

★★

THE new 'Cindy Crawford Workout Video' is bloody marvellous. I've only had it a fortnight and I've already got a right arm like Arnold Schwarzenegger.

B. Beater
St Anne's

★★

TOP TIP: Next time you have a large family gathering such as a wedding or birthday party don't invite Angela Lansbury. If she _does_ turn up, call the police, an ambulance and the coroner immediately.

S. Hammer, Bromsgrove

★★

IT'S coming to something when schoolchildren are asked to pay £6.50 for a guinea pig - £5.45 more than the advertised price. Pet shops nowadays are simply a law unto themselves.

Mrs Ann E.Bonnet
Fareham, Hants.

I WAS pleased to note that tea bag manufacturers are now attaching a piece of string and paper tag to tea bags to facilitate their retrieval should they accidentally be swallowed by children. If only other manufacturers would follow their lead.

Mrs Ruth Abbott
Hawes, North Yorkshire

★★★

TOP TIP: Top up your car battery with lemon juice. Not only does it have a high acid content, it will also add 'zest' to your engine's performance and leave your exhaust fumes smelling lemon fresh.

W. Sill, Frome

★★★

WHAT a rip-off these 'press on towels' are. It takes at least a dozen of them just to dry my arms.

R.Blackett
Peterlee

★★★

TOP TIP: Save hot water by going to bed at 6.30am with a hot water bottle. Get up an hour later and the water in the bottle will still be hot enough for a wet shave.

Mike Haworth, Manchester

★★★

ON a recent visit to the supermarket I found a purse and promptly handed it in at the office. It wasn't until I arrived at the checkout that I realised it was my own. I felt rather foolish as I returned to the office to collect it.

Mrs D.Carr
Surrey

AS a disabled driver I am fed up with other motorists parking on our designated spaces in supermarket car parks. Perhaps if the supermarkets would allocate us spaces in a far off corner of the car park, well away from the supermarket entrance, able bodied drivers would not be so tempted to park in them.

A. Smith
Putney

AFTER queuing overnight to grab some winter sale bargains at a local department store I was amazed and annoyed when a security guard refused to allow me inside the following morning. I soon realised why. I had camped in the doorway of the local cinema by mistake - the department store was on the opposite side of the street. Fortunately the cinema manager saw the funny side, and sold me a tub of popcorn for just 99p. (They usually cost a pound).

Penelope Rathbone-Harris
Kent

★★★

TOP TIP: German sex perverts. Rig up a four foot length of garden hose with a shower head on the end, drink ten pints of lager then attach the other end to your knob. Hey presto! Your own personalised golden shower!

A. Bain, Manchester

★★★

I HAD been trying for ages to give up nicotine patches, without success. Then the other day in the newsagents I came across some rolled fibrous sticks containing the same chemical, for inhalation. These 'ciggies' or 'tabs' are much cheaper than the patches, but have the same satisfying effect. They are widely available in a variety of brands and strengths.

T. Bensons
Nottingham

I USED to look forward to the odd evening when I would stay in and wash my hair. But since changing brands of shampoo to 'Wash & Go' I now feel obliged to go out immediately after every wash. I think shampoo manufacturers are inflicting unnecessary social pressure on women.

> Miss S. Head
> Lambeth

AFTER thinking about it for several days I eventually plucked up the courage to buy a couple of pornographic magazines, went into the shop and boldly asked for 'Mayfair' and 'Park Lane'.
"That will be £7 billion altogether", the man behind the counter said. Silly me. I had foolishly walked into an up market estate agents by mistake.

> Andrew Spind
> Chorley

★★★

TOP TIP: Save a fortune on laundry bills. Give your dirty shirts to Oxfam. They will wash and iron them and you can then buy them back for fifty pence.

> **J. B. Cartland, Brighton**

★★★

MY husband was delighted with the electric lawn mower we queued to buy in the January sales. He wasn't so pleased when I reminded him we don't have a lawn.

> Mrs J. Appleyard
> Ipswich

I'M a great believer in the saying 'you get what you pay for'. Not so at my local department store. I ordered a double bed and paid for it there and then. And they tell me it won't be delivered until Thursday.

> P. Hand
> Kingston

People Say The Funniest Things

NAPOLEON once described Britain as 'a nation of shop-keepers'. That's nonsense. My father is a plumber, and has been for 48 years.

Duncan Watson
Preston

THEY say that the grass is always greener on the other side of the fence. My neighbour would probably disagree, as I recently had my entire garden concreted over.

B. Bounty
Rochester

★★★

TOP TIP: When embarking on a new relationship always lend your partner twenty quid. That way, when you inevitably get chucked, at least you get your money back thus cheering up an otherwise miserable day.

A. Rolph, Chelmsford

★★★

"IT was somewhat fortunate for Father Christmas that Jesus was born in winter when there is lots of snow around for his sleigh", remarked my plucky four year old daughter the other day. "Imagine the damage to slates and the cost of replacing the metal runners every five minutes due to them being dragged over dry rooftops, had our Saviour been born in, say, mid July", she added.

Mr G. Green
London N15

WHO said cats have nine lives? It only took one sharp blow with a mallet to send my little 'Tiddles' to that great feline graveyard in the sky.

Edna Fowcett
Birkenhead

★★

TOP TIP: Prevent your ears from being bitten off in the pub by Sellotaping them flat to the side of your head.

P. Ash, Kent

★★

CHILDREN say the funniest things, and often at the most awkward moments. The other day I was invited to Buckingham Palace to receive a medal from the Queen.
"Where shall I stick it?" she asked, wondering where to pin the medal.
"Up your arse", said my 5 year old son, quick as a flash. My face went bright purple, and not surprisingly, I wasn't given the medal after all.

Mrs T. Hibbitt
Leeds

★★

TOP TIP: Left over Christmas tree 'needle drop' spray can be used on pets to prevent them dropping hairs on the carpet.

P. Cherry, Avon

★★

"LOOK, daddy is on fire!" said my daughter recently after my husband had lit up his pipe. We all laughed - except my husband that is. He believes that my 29 year old daughter's juvenile behaviour is the cause for some concern.

Mrs P. Ratnor
Billingham

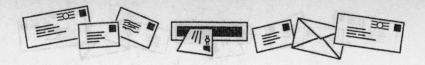

HOW many times have we heard the expression 'curiosity killed the cat'. Well it didn't. My next door neighbour did.

Linda Longbottom
Walsall

THE other day my 3-year-old son was in the bath when he suddenly cried out "Mummy. Come and look at my cock." Imagine my surprise and relief when I discovered he was referring to a small plastic cockerel belonging to his toy farm set, which he had taken into the bath with him!

Mrs N. Bluebird
Washington

★★★

TOP TIP: Star Trek captains. When your ship is in imminent danger of being destroyed, save a great deal of hassle by thinking of the last thing you could possibly try, which might just work, and do that first.

J.L. Pickard, Space

★★★

A FRIEND once told me the most dangerous part of a car is 'the nut behind the steering wheel'. Following his advice I removed this nut from my car. Later whilst travelling at speed on a dual carriageway the steering wheel became detached, and the car spun across the central reservation and collided head-on with an oncoming lorry. I was killed instantly. It just goes to show, you shouldn't believe everything people tell you.

T. Rodgers
Arbroath

THEY say 'every cloud has a silver lining'. That's nonsense. Clouds consist of condensed moisture, and the presence of silver is a physical impossibility.

R. Twig
Southend

"I'M playing with my knob", shouted my 3-year-old son whilst having a bath the other day. Imagine my relief to discover the knob in question was a round, wooden one which he had removed from the bathroom door!

Mrs N. Bluebird
Washington

★★

TOP TIP: Discourage pigeons from sitting on your roof by tethering a cat to the TV aerial.

Roger Radio, Faversham

★★

THE Bible tells us that it is easier for a camel to pass through the eye of a needle than it is for a rich man to enter the Kingdom of Heaven. Well, that's Cliff Richard buggered then, isn't it.

Mr I. Lancer
Croydon

"MUMMY. Look at the size of my pork sword", said my 3-year-old son the other day whilst playing in the bath. Imagine my relief upon entering the room to see him playing with a toy cutlass which he had somehow made out of sausages. Do I win £5?

> Mrs N. Bluebird
> Washington

★★★

TOP TIP: Restring that old tennis racket with piano wire. Hey presto! A "chipper" for potatoes, carrots, boiled eggs etc. which also allows you to practice your serve whilst cooking.

> **John Tait, Thropton**

★★★

WHILE travelling to work on the bus the other day I over-heard two old dears discussing their husbands. "Do you mind?" said one of them. "This happens to be a private conversation".

> Mrs E. Eales
> Liverpool

★★★

TOP TIP: Galaxy 'Minstrels' joined together by a cocktail stick would make a perfect set of dumb-bells for a squirrel, if they were a bit bigger. And heavier.

> **Leigh Loveday, Tamworth**

★★★

IT makes me laugh when people say 'an Englishman's home is his castle'. I live in a one bedroom council flat in Ripon. Then again I'm Welsh.

> Rhys Thomas
> Ripon

THEY say that the best way to a man's heart is through his stomach. That's absolute nonsense, and I should know. I am a heart surgeon, and the method I use is to make an incision in the thorassic cavity, bypass the myocardium, and once inside the rib cage it's a simple matter of removing the pericardium, and hey presto! There it is.

Dr David Williams
Standish

★★

TOP TIP: Don't waste hundreds of pounds having that tattoo of an ex-girlfriend's name removed from your arm by laser surgery. Simply give your new girlfriend £51 and she can have her name changed legally by deed poll to the name on the tattoo.

D. Kisilevsky
South Kensington

★★

TO say that the whole country has gone to the dogs is something of an exaggeration. I went for a night out at my local greyhound stadium last night and in the course of the entire evening I counted less than 300 spectators.

Matthew Cope
Swindon

★★

TOP TIP: Create instant designer stubble by sucking a magnet and dipping your chin in a bowl of iron filings.

B. Vilbens, Birmingham

★★

ACCORDING to feminists 'all men are potential rapists'. Well I'm not. I'm a convicted one.

G.B., HM Prison
Hull

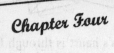

Chapter Four

Points Of You

IF the people who make Fairy Liquid simply diluted the stuff they wouldn't have to spend all that money on TV adverts telling people how strong it is.

Y. Bell
Norfolk

I'M in favour of the 24 hour clock. Imagine how much more work we'd get done in a day, and still have a lie in to boot.

Mr Loudhead
Cheadle Hume

★★

TOP TIP: Problems storing your CDs? Hang cotton threads from the ceiling and close your CD cases around them to produce your very own walk-through library. It also doubles as an interesting mobile for young children.

Greig Harper, Co. Durham

★★

IF I eat a sausage, wait several hours then sit on the toilet, a turd comes out of my bottom. Should it not therefore be the case that if I eat a turd and wait a few hours then sit on the toilet, a sausage would come out of my bum?

S. Bowyer
Trowbridge

I THINK the Royal Family are marvellous. They do a wonderful job.

Miss L. Hammond
Suffolk

WITH so many foreign football clubs naming themselves after electricity, such as AC Milan and Dynamo Kiev, isn't it about time English clubs followed suit? I for one would be proud to support Manchester Capacitors, Aston Fusewire or Wolverhampton Integrated Circuit Breakers.

The Manager
Tandy, Cheshunt, Herts.

★★

TOP TIP: A bicycle pump used backwards makes a handy makeshift vacuum cleaner.

T. Elm, Hornchurch, Essex.

★★

WHAT a wonderful sight those page 3 girls are. They certainly brighten up my mornings. My favourite is Samantha Fox, because she's got the biggest tits.

A. Belch
Poole

PERHAPS all your readers could donate a pound each to the government of Tahiti so that they can purchase a nuclear bomb of their own. They can then test it off the south of France, and give those frogs a taste of their own medicine.

Rich, Matt, Paul and Ian
Plymouth

I THINK that Kenneth Clarke deserves a pat on the back. In a day when politicians are clamouring to have affairs with dolly birds and MPs are often judged on the looks of their wives, it was nice to see that Mr Clarke thinks enough of his old mum to take her along to his budget day speech.

J. Doughnut
Feltham Abbey

I STILL think the Royal Family are marvellous and that they do a wonderful job.

Mrs L. Hammond
Suffolk

PEOPLE say that smoke-free workplaces are healthier and more productive. Nonsense. My boss banned smoking at work, and within a week everybody had been laid off, as we worked in a kipper factory.

L. Curd
Craster

AS I was walking to the shops the other day with my five year old daughter a lorry driver 'beeped' his horn at me and shouted "Phoar! Look at the tits on that!" It was a sunny day and I was wearing a short skirt at the time.

With so many miserable faces in the world these days, wouldn't it be nice if a few more people were as friendly as this a little more often.

Miss B. Idiot
Stoke on Trent

WHILE watching the snooker on TV last week I was surprised to hear the commentator say that young Stephen Hendry was going to clear the table. How nice it is to know that despite his rise to stardom and the huge sums of money he already earns, this sensible young man is still prepared to do his share of routine household chores. He should be an example to us all.

G. Ingram
Bristol

★★★

TOP TIP: Career women. Save time getting ready for work in the mornings by putting on five pairs of knickers on Monday. Then each morning simply whip off the top pair and hey presto! There's a clean pair underneath.

S. Stain, London

★★★

I THINK it's wonderful that the Welsh have a language all of their own. It gives them a sense of identity and enables them to keep in touch with their roots. It also means that us normal people don't have to talk to them.

A. Stapleton
Walthamstow

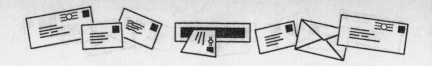

WHENEVER I see pubic hairs stuck to my soap bar I smile. We normal folk should be thankful that we have so much hair to spare. Just think of all the poor bald people whose heads will be getting cold this winter.

C. Litter
Ryhope

★★★

TOP TIP: Motorists. When asking for directions from a woman always look for one with small tits as they've usually got more brains. God seldom gives them both.

G. Kiss, Crawley

★★★

THINKING about religion the other day it occurred to me that not only was Jesus born on a bank holiday, but he also died on a bank holiday. I wouldn't claim to know what the Good Lord's next move is going to be, but it would seem a fair bet that the Second Coming will also be on a bank holiday.

P. G. Johnson
Long Eaton

★★★

TOP TIP: Make motorists sweat for up to ten days. Sit inside a cardboard box on top of a stick at the side of the road and take a flash photo of every car as it goes past.

Alan Currie, Wylam

★★★

ANY young girls thinking of getting married, take a word of advice. Don't marry anyone with big feet. If you do your children will have big feet too.

A. Everett
Brighton

IT'S true that money can't buy you happiness. Take the Queen, for example. She's got seven billion quid, and just look at the face on the miserable old cow.

F. Cortina
Dagenham

IT seems rather fashionable to 'have a go' at the Queen these days. With her vast personal fortune of £7 billion, her enormous income, her vast stable of racing horses, hundreds of servants and any number of stately homes, she's an easy target for the 'knockers'. But the Queen has a very difficult job to do, and I for one would not wish to swap places with her.

Mr J. Connors
Wembley

★★

TOP TIP: Girls. Don't worry about buying a new dress for that important first date. All he's interested in is seeing you starkers.

I. Cadman, Rotherham

★★

COULD I, if I may, take this opportunity to thank the young lady with a torch who showed me to my seat in the cinema last night. If it had not been for this kind person I may well have tripped and fallen in the dark.

It is perhaps a sad reflection of modern society that out of 300 people in the cinema only one person offered to help. Nevertheless, my heartfelt thanks go to her.

Mrs D. McLean
Eaglescliffe.

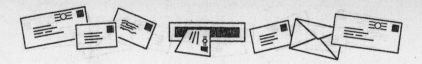

FURTHER to my previous letter. Having spent a few minutes thinking about it I've changed my mind. Yes, I would now be prepared to swap places with the Queen. The jammy old bitch.

Mr J. Connors
Wembley

★★★

TOP TIP: Always buy check shirts for your husband. Any food stains can then be accurately located using grid references.

Kevin Gildea, Ilford, Essex

★★★

THESE rising mortgage rates don't bother me at all. I'm a Brazilian, and consequently don't have to pay back money which I borrow from the bank.

Jesus Carambos Iguana
Cricklewood

★★★

TOP TIP: Jelly from pork pies, once warmed up, can be easily spread using a brush and is an economical substitute for varnish on doors, cupboards and skirting boards.

Lee & Dogs, Cleveland

★★★

WHAT is the point of testing nuclear bombs underground? We don't fight wars there. Why not test them in real conditions, like over Paris or Belgium.

D. Bull
Devon

Chapter Five

≡ LETTERBOCKS

Family Misfortunes

MY husband believes you should live every day as though it is your last. Consequently he has spent the last 17 years lying on his bed, attached to a saline drip, wearing an oxygen mask and with a rubber tube stuck up his arse.

Mrs T. Bolus
Spittle

MY hubby never listens to a word I say. Hardly surprising, as he ran off with another woman 25 years ago and now lives in Canada.

Mrs Myte
London

★★

TOP TIP: Prolong the life of leather underpants by spraying them with 'Scotch Guard' before use.

N. Thorpe, Hockley

★★

AFTER eight weeks receiving treatment in a local private hospital my father died from a serious heart condition. To my amazement, a week later the hospital sent me a bill. If a local garage had completely written off my car instead of repairing it I doubt if they'd have been so quick to send me a bill.

Mrs I. Jones
Blackheath

TALK about the power of television! While vacuuming the carpet the other day my wife accidentally severed a cable connecting our TV set to the mains - and she was killed instantly.

Mr C. Deeley
Birmingham

I DIDN'T know what to think walking into the kitchen last night to find my wife draped in lasagna and pouring piping hot soup over her head.
"I'm just putting the dinner on", she quipped. How we laughed on the way to the burns unit.

A Hampton
Hampton.

TOP TIP: Mums. Add sparkling mineral water to a tin of condensed soup, then heat. Hey presto! Fizzy soup that your kids will adore.

Rowland Lee, Nottingham

RAT of the Week must surely be whoever stole my elderly mother while she slept in her wheelchair outside the Lea Rig public house some time between 1.00pm and 10.30pm last Thursday. The cheeky thief struck as I sat only yards away, playing dominoes with friends in the bar.

Is the rodent heartened to learn that I was forced to stay at home all weekend, as mother's pension book was in her pocket?

'Disgusted'
Dundee

CAN any of your readers help us trace our grandmother Mrs Ethel Stubbs of Waterloo Place, North Shields. She was last seen at Preston Cemetery being lowered into the ground in a coffin.

Robert & Peter Bertram
Liverpool

★★

TOP TIP: Save money on expensive boiled sweets. Give the kiddies frozen grapes to suck. They're just as sweet, cheaper to buy, and much lower on calories.

Ian Budd, Manchester

★★

A RATHER handsome postman called at our door with a package addressed to 'Mrs P Wall'. "Is your mother in?" he asked when I opened the door. His remark made my day. He obviously thought I was too young to be married. For a moment I was flattered, until I remembered I am in fact 12, and the parcel was *indeed* for my mother.

Mary Wall
Wallington

LAST night my wife worked late and her kind-hearted boss invited her back to his house for a meal. He even treated her to a bottle of champagne. How generous it was of him - rarely do you hear of such kindly behaviour by an employer these days.

My wife however must have felt pretty foolish. For on her return, I pointed out that she had been wearing her dress inside out.

R. W.
L. icester

★★★

TOP TIP: Burglars. Spend half an hour in a hot bath before you do your next 'job'. After a good soak the police will never be able to identify your crinkly fingerprints or 'dabs'.

Thora Pee, Pontefract

★★★

THEY say 'no news is good news'. Well, my grandfather went on a two week camping holiday in Zambia in 1952 and hasn't been seen since. So I hardly think the saying applies in this case.

C. Woestmann
Hollywood

MY husband had always dreamt of being a professional foot-baller. But after serving in the merchant navy during the war and then on the railways, he ended up working in insurance until his recent retirement. But now, at 68, he has taken up football again. He has been in training for over a month, and has written to several clubs asking for a trial.

It only goes to show - you're never too old to change your career.

Mrs E. Brookes
Brinkley

WHILE out playing football recently my 68-year-old husband suffered a heart attack and died. Let this be a warning to other elderly folk. Too much exercise, especially in later life, can be a dangerous thing.

Mrs E. Brookes
Brinkley

★★★

TOP TIP: Joyriders. Lie in the freezer all day before going out at nights to steal cars. Then, when you ditch the motor and run for it through people's back gardens, you'll be invisible to the thermal imaging cameras on the police helicopter.

Urinal Dockrat
Marsworth, Bucks

★★★

THEY say 'a watched pot never boils'. What nonsense. My wife filled a pot with water and I sat and watched it boil in exactly 4 minutes 35 seconds.

Ian Goodall
Camden

★★★

TOP TIP: Avoid endless arguments with your wife about leaving the toilet seat down by simply pissing in the sink.

A. Toplight, Neville Hill

★★★

MY husband, mistaking the local remand home for a TV repair shop, strode in and asked a group of unruly youths if they'd like to come home with him and have a look at his knob which hadn't been turning on properly. I visited him in hospital yesterday where he remains in a critical condition, and has so far been unable to see the funny side of the incident.

Mrs B. Evans
Berwick

I AM worried about my son. The other night he said he was going out with some friends to paint the town red. The following morning he awoke complaining of a dreadful headache and was unable to go to college. I wonder whether perhaps this could have been caused by the paint fumes?

Mrs P. Brown
Shrewsbury

★★★

TOP TIP: Keep your wife on her toes. Nail the housekeeping money to the ceiling.

S. Round, Paignton

★★★

MY father is living proof of the saying 'You're never too old to marry'. When my mother died thirty years ago he moved into a rest home. Fifty-two years later he remarried. He is now 187 and I have forty-eight lovely grandchildren.

Mrs K. Emmerson
Huddersfield

★★★

TOP TIP: Create an 'Arctic' scene for your white mice by covering the floor of their cage in talcum powder instead of sawdust, and building a small igloo using sugar cubes.

Dr M. Best, Loughborough

★★★

I'D like to get my hands on the pop star who recorded the song 'White Lines Don't Do It'. My son decided to take his advice, and ended up getting the sack from his job. He worked for the council painting white lines in the middle of the road.

Mr D. Kennel
Hull

MY husband is a real outdoor survival expert. For the last three months he has lived in a den on a riverbank, and eaten nothing but fish which he catches himself by diving underwater.

Mind you, he is an otter.

Mrs Otter
River Exe, Devon

AS a senior citizen, 88 years young and not a day in hospital, I am often asked by my children and grandchildren what is the secret of a long, healthy life. I always give the same answer. "If I told you, it wouldn't be a secret anymore. So mind your own business".

Mrs P. J. Gooland
London N4

★★★

TOP TIP: Pot holers. Save the emergency services time and money by pot holing in your own bathroom at night. With the lights off, crawl through a bath full of water, under the sink, then get your head stuck in the toilet. Wait till morning for your wife to wake up and 'rescue' you.

J. Moss, Washington

★★★

AS a married man I used to fantasise about the thrill of having sex with a prostitute, but I never dared try it. Well now I get the best of both worlds. First, I put a red bulb in my wife's bedside lamp, then I told her to chew gum and appear disinterested during sex. She charges me £20 for hand relief (£30 topless), and £50 for full sex. Our love life has never been so exciting. In order to add a little extra authenticity my 18 year old son acts as her 'pimp', calling her his 'bitch', keeping most of the money and interrupting our 'sessions' if they run slightly over time.

Mr S. Birch
Croydon

AMERICAN singer song-writer Neil Sedaka told us that "Breaking up is hard to do". The facts of the matter are that one marriage in four now ends in divorce, a figure which leaves Mr Sedaka looking rather stupid. To avoid further embarrassment perhaps he should consult the statisticians before making any future records.

M. Desk
Longbenton

★★★

TOP TIP: Disturbed American teenagers. Develop a more balanced perspective on life by listening to Ozzie Osborne's 'Suicide Solution' immediately followed by Queen's 'Don't Try Suicide'.

Boogie, Rhonda

★★★

WOULD it not be an idea for vicars to take a leaf out of the FA's book, and appoint a 'referee' to officiate over new marriages. Dressed in black shirt and shorts, he could blow a whistle when he felt either partner had committed an offence, and caution them for serious misconduct. As a last resort he could 'send off' one or other partner, thus ending the marriage. Like football referees these men could be simple, and therefore relatively cheap to employ.

D. Matheson
Cambridge

EXPERTS fear that eating beef products containing brain or spinal chord may cause 'mad cow disease' to develop in our children in 10 or 20 years time. I therefore refuse to allow my children to eat these bits. Instead I give them to my mother, who is 87, and won't be around in a year or two anyway.

Irene Saddleworth
Buckstead

'EARLY to bed, early to rise, makes a man healthy, wealthy and wise'. Try telling that to my father. He's a postman, goes to bed at 9pm every night and gets up at 3am. He's dying of cancer, owes a loan company £5,000, and has never finished The Sun crossword in his life, despite trying every day since 1969.

Mr Lights
Dollar

★★★

TOP TIP: Frozen drop scones make handy coasters for hot drinks. By the time you finish your drink, the scones should have thawed and will be warm enough to add hot butter and jam.

N. Thorpe, Hockley

★★★

"YOU soon begin to realise your children are growing up" a friend told me, "when their feet get bigger and you have to buy them new shoes".

P. Martin
Southport

★★★

TOP TIP: Housewives. Brighten up Mondays by coating your kitchen floor with 'Quavers' in order to recreate the sound of walking through virgin snow whilst preparing the tea.

Mrs T., Thropton

★★★

MY wife and I have been together now for over fifty years, but I will never forget the day we married. It was a Saturday.

M. Error
Battersea

Chapter Six

Road and Rail Rage

BRITISH RAIL say 'we're getting there'. Well I disagree. During the recent wintry weather I waited for 4 days at my local station with no sign of any trains. Only when the snow melted did I realise the station had been closed several years ago and the track removed. Needless to say there had been no announcements to this effect, and not one member of staff was anywhere to be seen.

M. Scott-Jarvis
Redesmouth

★★

TOP TIP: Keep postie on his toes by making six different shaped letter boxes in your front door (square, circle, star, rectangle etc.) and posting yourself six correspondingly shaped parcels for him to deliver.

M. Cooper, Leyland

★★

ONE evening I noticed that the train was unusually slow travelling home from work. Imagine my surprise to find that I had taken a seat inside the local cinema opposite the railway station, by mistake. This explained why my ticket price had suddenly risen from the usual £1.10 to £2.75, and the buffet appeared to be serving nothing but ice creams and popcorn.

S. Konker
Bristol

AREN'T traffic wardens a miserable lot. I shouted colourful abuse at one the other day, hoping to raise a smile. If you'd seen the look on his face you'd have thought the world was coming to an end! I realise they have a difficult job to do, but what on Earth have people got against smiling?

Ken Higgins
Deptford

LOOKING through the Highway Code the other day I was unable to find the rule which tells London bus drivers to pull out into the road whilst still occupied with taking money from passengers, having indicated their intention to do so for at least three minutes beforehand. Perhaps my edition is a misprint.

P. J. Taylor
Amersham

★★

TOP TIP: Diffuse 'road rage' stand-offs by out-stretching your arms and suggesting that you both hug.

Austin Fisher, Finsbury Park

★★

ON my way to work this morning the train I was travelling in narrowly missed colliding with over a dozen trains travelling in the opposite direction. We often hear about 'near misses' involving aeroplanes. I trust that similar incidents involving trains are being reported to the appropriate authorities.

Scared
Wokingham

I TRY to avoid using trains whenever possible, as the service is invariably poor. On a recent journey from Bristol to London my train eventually arrived, over 7 hours late - in Aberdeen.

B. Bradham
Bristol

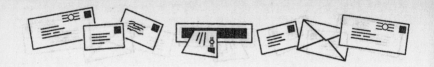

I AM increasingly fed up with British Railways. On a recent journey I spent over three hours trying to find the buffet, only to be told that there wasn't a buffet car on the train. By this time I had missed my stop, and was forced to pay £140 for a taxi home.

G. Hamilton
Cheshire

★★

TOP TIP: Wheelie bins left at the gate make ideal shopping trolleys for burglars.

John Tait, Thropton

★★

THE problem with public transport is not the cost, geographical availability, frequency or efficiency of the services provided. It is the fact that a high proportion of people who use it smell.

M. Thigh
Cambridge

WHY do police and magistrates always come down so hard on motorists who have accidents after they have been drinking. Clearly having had a few drinks a person's ability to drive is greatly reduced. It is the *sober* motorists, who despite *not* drinking, still manage to crash their cars, who the authorities ought to be clamping down on.

D. McLure
Arbroath

I DON'T know what all the fuss is about drink/driving. I drink/drive every day. I'm a dray man for the local brewery, and drive drink to dozens of pubs each week.

B. McCannel
Portstewart

P.S. Come to think of it I do drink quite a lot of it as well.

★★

TOP TIP: Farting in bed a problem? Before you hit the sack, try popping a Mint Imperial up your Marmite motorway. That way your guffs will smell good enough to eat.

Sue Denim, London NW1

★★

IT seems ridiculous to waste the police's time expecting them to catch speeding motorists. I'm sure they have far better things to do. Why not replace traffic police with a simple 'honesty box' situated on every car's dashboard. Motorists could then pay 10p every time they exceed the speed limit, and a pound if they do more than 100 miles per hour. The system could also be used to penalise slower drivers who get in other people's way. They could pay an extra 50p every time they are overtaken.

H. Balderstone-Smythe
Newmarket

FUNNY how passengers are expected to pay for their journeys on public transport and yet drivers always travel for free. I'm sure that if these so-called 'train drivers' had to pay the same exorbitant price for a ticket that we do, they'd make *damn* sure the train arrived on time.

Mr T. Hodgson
Essex

I SPOTTED this slightly amusing car registration number in a car park recently. Do I win £5?
    D. Wheeler
    Thornaby

WELL, how about this one then?
    D. Wheeler
    Thornaby

I WAS driving to work this morning when I saw a sign on the back of a bus. It read, *"Are you reading this advertisement? Then so are your customers"*. I had to laugh, because I am a travelling salesman and I sell white sticks and guide dogs to the blind.

N. Walters
London

DRIVING home the other day I was unable to get a decent reception on my car radio so I decided to whistle my favourite tune instead. Imagine my disappointment when I arrived home before it had finished.

Granville Canty
Hebden Bridge

I HAVE a simple remedy to the problem of our overcrowded motorways. Why not allow people in the upper tax bracket only to drive in the outside lane. And during the rush hour drivers whose cars are more than five years old would have to pull in onto the hard shoulder. The problem of congestion would be cured at a single stroke.

H. Balderstone-Smythe
Newmarket

★★★

TOP TIP: Housewives. When making hubby's sandwiches for work, always fill one with toothpaste. Make sure he eats this one last, for healthier teeth and gums.

M. Bike, Berkshire

★★★

THEY say that an area of rain forest equivalent to the size of Wales is dug up every day. If it's that easy, why don't they simply dig up Wales? It would only take a day, and in its place they could build a car park for people visiting Cheshire.

I. Alerstone
Nantwich

I WAS bitterly disappointed when Ford decided to name their new car the 'Mondeo', breaking with the popular trend of naming them after adult 'wank' mags, like Fiesta and Escort. I had hoped to see a new Ford Razzle, or a Ford Readers' Wives Bums Special.

Stan Drews
St Andrews

NOW that the AA is advertising itself as the 'fourth emergency service' perhaps we can look forward to a TV drama like Casualty, The Bill or London's Burning. Stranded motorists wait on the hard shoulder for five hours until a spotty youth in a van with disco lights on the top arrives. Then he tows them to a garage for a £150 service simply because they've run out of petrol. I'm sure it would be popular viewing.

R. A. Coates
Blackpool

★★

TOP TIP: Dirty carpets? Make your own 'Hoover' by fixing door draft excluder brushes to the blades of an old petrol lawn mower.

Sam Brairo, Truro

★★

I BECAME concerned recently when a group of burly youths clambered aboard my bus carrying baseball bats. Until I remembered - I am the team manager for the New York Yankees.

F. Nosejob
New York

★★

TOP TIP: A ball of Edam cheese with the centre carefully removed makes an ideal crash helmet for mountain bikers.

J. Ouster, Isle of Man

★★

I MUST admit, since British Rail changed the colour of their trains and started referring to passengers as 'customers' I've completely forgotten what an abysmal and over priced service they provide.

T. Lock
Liverpool

I HAVE often wondered why multi-storey car parks smell of piss. I recently found out. After drinking heavily all day on New Year's Eve I staggered back to the car park where I thought I had left my car. After several minutes spent fruitlessly searching for the vehicle I became dizzy and decided to sit down for a rest in the stairwell. The next thing I knew it was three o'clock in the afternoon on New Year's Day and I awoke sitting in a puddle of my own urine. Funnily enough when I eventually returned home my wife reminded me that our car had been in the garage since I crashed it into a lamp post on Christmas Eve.

D. Fir
Hull

★★

TOP TIP: Office workers. Top up that fading holiday tan during quiet moments by lying naked on the photocopier and pressing the 'copy' button.

Mark Anderson, Hampstead

★★

WITH so many fights taking place in pub car parks would it not be an idea to ban pubs from having car parks, especially as you are not supposed to drink and drive nowadays. The money saved could be used to build hospitals for orphans, guide dogs for the blind or walking sticks for the elderly.

V. Gray
Bedminster, Bristol

THE vast majority of road traffic accidents happen within three miles of the driver's home. I therefore reduce my risk of crashing by keeping my car in a lock-up garage three miles away, and travelling to and from the garage by bicycle. Once in my car I can drive as recklessly as I like with little or no danger of crashing.

D. Turner
Canterbury

THE Government proposes to invest millions of pounds in complex electronic equipment to facilitate the automatic payment of tolls by drivers using our motorways. Would it not be cheaper and more practical to employ the system successfully operated on fairground dodgem cars for many years, and simply pay tattooed youths to clamber from one car to another demanding a cash payment from the driver.

E. Bainbridge
Walthamstow

★★

TOP TIP: Ignore signs in hotel bathrooms telling you to put the shower curtain inside the bath. It takes 28 minutes to get the hooks off.

J. B. Cartland, Brighton

★★

I DECIDED to try this new form of smash and grab robbery they call 'ram raiding', and drove to a local off license, ploughing the car in through the shop window before making off with liquor and cigarettes. I thought my raid had been a success when I totted up my haul later - over £1000's worth of stolen goods. But the next day I got a bill from the garage for the damage to my car - it cost £1800 just to have it repaired! I think I'll stick to conventional burglaries in future.

A. Smith
Gateshead

★★

TOP TIP: For many years I've kept my legs warm in winter by wearing ladies' tights beneath my trousers. I've never found it embarrassing, as they make perfectly good - and economical - leg warmers. As a pensioner saving money and staying warm are my priorities. In summer I switch to wearing cooler and more hygienic stockings and suspenders.

Mr A. Cream, Rotherham

★★

★★★

TOP TIP: Road rage drivers. Settle your dispute honourably by removing your car aerials and having a fencing duel. The aerials will retract if they hit a solid object, thus preventing serious injury.

Pete Doolan, Yeovil

★★★

IMAGINE how many hospitals we could build with all the money we'd save by doing away with traffic lights. Just think of all the electricity they waste shining away when half the time no-one is even looking at them. Surely a simpler way to control traffic at junctions would be for motorists to take turns at having right of way. If you waited at one junction, then you'd have right of way at the next, etc. As well as saving money, this would also help create a more friendly, co-operative atmosphere among road users.

P. Limpet
Coventry

★★★

TOP TIP: Weather men. Save a fortune in meteorological expenses by simply saying that the weather will be the same as it was the day before. More often than not you'll be right.

P. Beading, Cleveland

★★★

I HAVE been driving for over forty years and never indicated left or right in all that time. Why should I? It's nobody's business but my own where I'm going. I don't care where the person in front of me is going. He could be going to Timbuktu for all I care. So why should I have to tell the person behind me where I'm going? He can jolly well mind his own business.

R. Heart
Reading

Chapter Seven

It's A Funny Old World

YESTERDAY my teenage son arrived home from school early and caught me parading in front of our bedroom mirror wearing high heels, ladies underwear, a dress and make-up. I almost died of embarrassment, until I remembered - I'm his mother.

Mrs T. Tank-Engine
Sodor

I WAS saying to friend that it seemed like only yesterday we'd huddled around a TV set to watch England beat Germany in the 1966 World Cup final. I felt a proper fool when he reminded me *it was*. We'd watched the match on video the previous evening.

D. Turner
Canterbury

★★★

TOP TIP: Chefs. When fixing together the pieces of a broken cake dry pasta spirals make perfect 'screws'.

J.T., Morpeth

★★★

MY wife and I went on holiday to Spain last year. On our first night we were amazed to meet our next door neighbours in the hotel bar! Until we remembered - we had invited them on holiday with us.

M. Baker
Barnstable

AN insurance form asked whether I have any valuable antiques in my house. "Only you, eh dear?" I joked with my wife. She's 96, and her gold teeth are probably worth more than our entire house contents. Luckily she didn't hear my remark. She's as deaf as a post.

D. P. Course
Evesham

★★

TOP TIP: Give your clothes that 'Elvis sparkle' by allowing a snail to crawl all over you.

J. Elvis, Jarrow

★★

MY dad, a heavy smoker, was determined that I wouldn't follow in his footsteps. So when he caught me smoking at the age of 14 he forced me to eat an ashtray full of cigarette ends. It worked - and I haven't smoked a cigarette since, although I am often thrown out of pubs for going around the tables eating the contents of the ashtrays.

Mark Smith
Stambourne, Essex

★★

TOP TIP: Give yourself an 'Elvis style' lip by knotting a piece of cotton thread and lodging it between your two front teeth, pulling it tight and then wrapping the other end several times around your ear.

B. Idol, Hospital, Hollywood

★★

I RECENTLY misread an 'OFFICE TO LET' sign as 'OFFICE TOILET' and relieved myself through the letter box.

Mrs P. Nilewart
Leeds

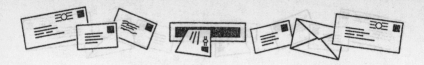

I WAS convinced my husband was having an affair with his secretary, as he often returned home late from work smelling of perfume. So the other night I confronted him. I felt such a fool when he reminded me he doesn't have a secretary - he works as a forklift truck driver at the local perfume factory, and has recently been working evening shifts.

Mrs C. Kettledrum
Filey

PEOPLE are always telling me that my dog looks like Mother Teresa of Calcutta. I wonder whether any other readers have pets which resemble former Nobel Peace Prize winners?

Neil Hargreaves
Blackburn

TOP TIP: Read 'Exchange & Mart' from cover to cover while sitting on the toilet. When you eventually get up and try to walk on your numbed legs you will find your legs swaying and gyrating, just like Elvis.

F. Starr, A pub somewhere

I REALLY can't see the need for all this fuss about corn circles. On a farm near to where I live the aliens have cut down all the crops, rolled them into enormous cylinder shapes, and stacked them all neatly at the side of the fields. None of the local residents, including myself, have felt it necessary to bat an eyelid.

Mr J. Bright
Sheppey, Kent

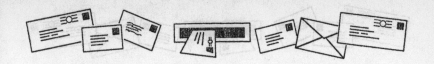

MY boss sent me to collect some glasses for him the other day. After visiting every opticians in town my mistake suddenly dawned on me. I'm a barmaid, and the *glasses* he wanted me to collect were empty beer glasses from around the tables in his pub. How he laughed when he realised what I'd done, before sacking me on the spot.

> G. Canty (Miss)
> Hebden Bridge

ON the subject of pet look-alikes, people often remark on the amazing likeness between my ewe (pictured) and Channel Four's John McCrirrick. Can readers spot the likeness?

> Claire Smith
> Tadcaster

★★★

TOP TIP: Ravers. Pop a wooden spoon in your mouth when dancing. This will eliminate the risk of biting off your tongue in the event of an epileptic fit caused by strobe lighting, and will soon become a fashion item.

> **W. Brooks, Somerset**

★★★

AT my father's funeral the other day the bottom fell out of the coffin and the body smashed onto the marble church floor. Unfortunately the head became separated and rolled under one of the pews, whence it became stuck under a wooden panel. Everyone was in fits of laughter as the vicar took half an hour to retrieve the head using a candlestick. Even the undertaker couldn't keep a straight face. Had my father been alive, I'm sure he would have been laughing as loud as we were.

> D. Spruce
> Reading

I BEGAN drinking at the age of 16, and have been a chronic alcoholic for the last twenty years, spending a fortune each week on beer, lager and spirits. But come 'Comic Relief' I'm the one who's laughing, as I never have to waste my money on a silly plastic red nose. I already have one!

I. P. Head
Middlesbrough

★★★

TOP TIP: Mums. A strip of banana peel tacked to the bottom of children's shoes allows them to be towed effortlessly around supermarkets.

J. Tait, Thropton

★★★

"LOOKS like someone got out of bed on the wrong side this morning", said the paramedic after I had rolled off my bed and out of an adjacent window, landing in a greenhouse several floors below. To prevent similar mishaps my bed is now pushed firmly up against a wall on the opposite side of the bedroom!

P. Hamilton
Mile End, London

I GOT a phone call at work the other day from a next door neighbour who told me that the alarm had gone off, so I rushed back to my house to investigate. Only when I got there did I realise he was in fact referring to the pop group 'The Alarm'.

"They haven't made a decent record since *68 Guns*," he told me as I got out of my car.

R. Mattress
Hersham

MY pet gerbil Lionel is the spitting image of Palestinian leader Yasser Arafat. Do I win £10?

Sketty, Shanklin
I.O.W.

I AM 70 years old yet have never experienced a strange or amusing coincidence. Funnily enough neither has my brother.

F. Coyle
Hammersmith

WHEN I boarded a bus the other day I was sure I had seen the driver somewhere before. I remembered where when he turned up on my doorstep that evening. He was my husband.

Mrs D. McArdle
Arbroath.

'CATCHING a falling leaf brings 12 months of happiness', or so the saying goes. I ran to catch one last autumn, but looking up I tripped and fell under a bus. I managed to hold onto the leaf - just - but did it bring me 12 months happiness? It's hard to tell, as I died in hospital less than one month after the accident.

D. Dixon
Dumfries

I GOT a shock the other day when I arrived at work only to find the place had been reduced to a pile of rubble. I had to laugh when my boss reminded me - I'm a demolition engineer and we were busy demolishing an old power station.

B. Liar
Essex

AS a New Year's resolution I decided not smoke more than ten cigarettes a day. I thought I was doing really well until after a couple of weeks my wife pointed out that previously I had never smoked at all.
I think there's a lesson here for all of us.

Peter Owners-Manual
Haynes

RECENTLY my girlfriend finished with me, saying I was "Useless in the trouser department". Ironically enough, the following week I was sacked from my job as head trouser salesman in Marks and Spencers.

C. Perkins
Bristol

"I'M not at all well", I said to my wife as I sat with my head in my hands, my stomach turning. "I feel like a drunken passenger on a ship at sea".
"That is because you are", she replied. After drinking 24 pints of bitter I had forgotten we were on holiday aboard the QE2.

J. Begley
Timperley

"YOU treat this place like a bloody hotel, coming and going whenever it suits you", said my mother the other day. Imagine her embarrassment when she remembered she is a hotel receptionist, and she was talking to a guest who had just handed in his room key.

D. Collier
Nottingham

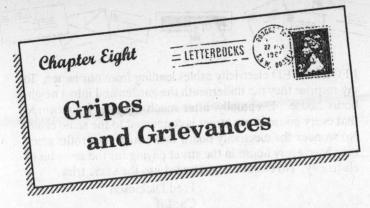

Gripes and Grievances

VICARS have it easy. They don't pay tax, they get a free house, they only work one day a week and then they have the check to pass the plate round on a Sunday looking for tips.

Mr T. Evans
Somerset

★★

TOP TIP: Catch a condor by simply building a wooden stockade 1 metre high and 50 metres in diameter, and then placing a dead goat in the centre. The bird will land inside the stockade to feed on the goat, but will then be unable to get out. This is because condors require a 'run up' of at least 100 metres before they can gain the momentum necessary for take off.

G. Hill, Birmingham

★★

WHAT a con these so called 'refillable' gas cigarette lighters are. My husband tried to refill his from our gas cooker, but after a couple of hours gave up and lit a match instead. In the resulting explosion the gable end of our house collapsed and my two year old fitted kitchen - for which I am still paying - was damaged beyond repair. They say cigarettes can harm your health. My husband would probably disagree and say that cigarette lighters cause more harm, had he not been killed in the explosion.

Mrs J. Chernock
Cheadle, Cheshire

I FOLLOWED electricity cables leading from our meter. To my surprise they ran underneath the garden and into a neighbours house. Eventually, after much digging, I discovered that every house in our street is connected to the same cable. No wonder the electricity board make such fat profits when they have every house in the street paying for the same bit of electricity. No doubt the gas board use the same trick.

Fred Dickinson
Cardiff

★★

TOP TIP: A stiff toothbrush makes an ideal comb for trendy sideburns.

Spencer D. Group
Wirral

★★

I GET hopping made when, during a visit to the cinema, almost all the audience get to their feet just before the end of the film and make a mad rush for the exit.
Now, if everyone did as I do and remained seated until everyone else had gone, there wouldn't be a mad rush.

J. A. Windridge
Stoke on Trent

IN the old days if we wanted to go out to a dance we had to wear my mother's bedroom curtains, and paint shoes on our feet using my grandad's army boot polish. And we had to be home by ten o'clock so that my mother could draw the curtains when she went to bed. I couldn't believe my ears last week when my grandson, who is two, asked for £600 to buy a pair of these modern 'training shoes' to wear in the pub. Has the world gone mad?

Mrs Ada Brady
Fulchester

I'M sick and tired of people going on about how horrible the war was. Well I was there, and it was bloody great. I rode on a motorbike, went in a plane, and shot three Germans. I had a marvellous time.

Tom Hobson
Sudbury

★★★

TOP TIP: Old folk. Keep your living room warm in winter by plugging in your electric iron and using it as a door stop.

Michael Harby, Bakewell

★★★

WHAT is it with posh people that they have to have two second names when everyone else makes do with one? People like Tiggy Legge-Bourke, Lucinda Prior-Palmer and Helen Melons-Windsor. Hats off to Prince Charles for trying to stop this elitist fashion by having no second name at all.

S. Cord
Laira

IF the only way to save trees is to have new age hippies clambering about building nests in them, I'm for chopping them all down and having roads instead.

Mr D. L. Infantry
Gateshead

I'M fed up with fishermen who go out in trawlers, catch net fulls of fish and then grumble about the size of their catch, claiming that they can't make a living. My grandad used to go fishing, and he'd be happy if he caught one fish, never mind a whole net full.

B. Bates
Nottingham

★★

TOP TIP: Catch a monkey by drilling a hole in a hollow tree just wide enough for a monkey's hand to pass through, then put nuts inside the hole. The monkey will stick his hand inside the tree to reach them, but with the nuts in his grasp his hand will be too wide to remove from the hole. The animal will not have the intelligence to drop the nuts in order to effect his escape.

G. Hill, Birmingham

★★

I'M fed up with these vegetarians who moan and bleat every time normal blokes like me go out and do a bit of hunting. If it wasn't for the likes of me the wildlife would eat all the lentils and sprouts and there'd be nothing left for the veggies. Then they'd all have to have sausages like everyone else.

D. Bruce
Colchester

I'M sick and tired of hearing old soldiers complaining about conditions working on the Burma to Siam Railway. They should try working for British Rail, taking home a poxy £146 a week, having to listen to middle class twats moaning because their train is a couple of hours late, and wearing an ill-fitting clowns uniform all day with absolutely no chance of getting a tan.

Ian Short
Watford

IF vegetarianism is such a good idea, how come vegetarians all have bad breath and fart a lot? If God had wanted us to eat grass, he'd have made us rabbits.

Tom Higgins
Swindon

ANYONE who thinks butterflies are beautiful should try pulling their over sized wings off. Without them they look just like any other disgusting insect.

Nick Allen
Sale, Cheshire

IT'S interesting to hear all the feminists wailing and cheering Lorena Bobbit for cutting off her husband's penis. But I bet it would be a different story if some poor battered husband had filled up his wife's crack with Polyfilla.

Will Pearson
Leicester

★★★

TOP TIP: Amaze your neighbours by tightrope walking across your clothes line without the use of a safety net. Simply thread the clothes line through short sections of hosepipe glued to the bottom of your shoes. Providing your shoe laces are tied tightly, falling off is impossible.

M. Board, Romney

★★★

SO the chairman of Yorkshire Water washes his hands, groin and feet using only one cupful of water? Big deal! I can clean my whole body, including my arse, using only my tongue, and no water at all. Mind you, I'm a cat.

Tiddles
Weybridge

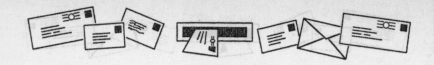

HOW come when I'm shagging my girlfriend she starts to whine cos I can only last two minutes? You'd think she'd take it as a compliment, the miserable cow.

Joel Young
Middlesbrough

I HAVE every sympathy with people who suffer from physical disabilities, but don't the architects realise that their grand notions of wheelchair access to all public buildings will leave the Earth wide open to invasion by Daleks or similar aliens from outer space?

Fred Thomas
Acton, W3

★★

TOP TIP: Toblerone chocolate bars make ideal 'toast racks' for Ritz crackers.

Max China, Kendal

★★

I'M all in favour of the Government forcing absent fathers to pay ludicrous amounts towards the maintenance of their children. It will make them think twice in future before having sex with a lesbian, which I believe most of these single parent mothers are. The rest are, of course, prostitutes, and perhaps they should be taxed on the money which the fathers no doubt paid them in the first place for having sex.

C. Pot
Clapham

I HOPE that the Bank of England will spare a thought for us swimming pool attendants when they next introduce a new coin. We rarely have time to empty our pockets before diving into pools, so it would assist us greatly - and possibly save lives - if new coins were lightweight and waterproof.

Bob Patterson
Manchester

WHY waste millions of pounds introducing more confusing new coins? If the Bank of England spent a small amount encouraging people to clean their existing coins, all our money would be nice and shiny and there would be no need for newly minted coins.

> Ethel Paynter
> Cheltenham

★★★

TOP TIP: Steel wool moistened with a drop of oil is ideal for wiping baby robots bottoms with.

> **J.T., Northumberland**

★★★

RATHER than arguing about whether or not the clocks should be brought forwards and backwards an hour every year, why don't we simply put them forward 12 hours permanently? This way pedestrians would be much safer on the roads at night, and there'd be a huge saving on electricity as street lights would no longer be required.

> R. Oldfield
> Clywd

★★★

TOP TIP: Old folk. Make mealtimes easier by employing a set of novelty clockwork teeth to 'pre-chew' your food before it enters your mouth.

> **J.T., Thropton**

★★★

WHATEVER happened to the Dunkirk spirit? The other day an old lady was attacked in broad daylight in our local high street. I stood and watched for a good five minutes during which time not a single person lifted a finger to help.

> L. Norder
> Camberly

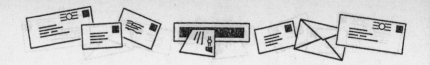

YOU can't trust anybody these days. The other day my neighbour nipped out to the shops. He was only gone ten minutes, but by the time he'd got back I'd broken into his house and stolen his TV, video, and hi-fi.

Steven Arthurs
Bristol

★★

TOP TIP: Girls. Stuff a pitta bread with tampons, lipstick, etc. Your friends will be green with envy at your 'Viviene Westwood' style clutch bag.

Bunny McMahon, Cork

★★

ONCE again we hear the sickening news that a pensioner has been beaten up in their own home by heartless thugs who stole a paltry 60p. How awful that a life can be shattered for such a trivial sum. It wouldn't be so bad if these people would steal a reasonable amount - say £50 or £60. And perhaps some jewellery.

A. Anderson
Hereford

★★

TOP TIP: Promise to ring people at specific times, then don't. They'll ring you to see what's wrong, at which point you can have your original planned conversation at their expense.

Dawn Ralphson, Lancs.

★★

WHAT a con these so called 'oven gloves' are. I recently poured a chicken casserole into mine. Two hours later I returned to find the casserole uncooked and a terrible mess all over my kitchen floor.

Peter Ring
Lancing, West Sussex

Chapter Nine

People Continue To Say *More* of the Funniest Things

THEY say you can't teach an old dog new tricks. Bollocks. I just taught my wife to juggle, and she's 52.

> Jay Cox
> Grays, Essex

OUR three year old grand-daughter is a constant source of amusement. "I wish you'd hurry up and die, you wrinkly old rat bag, and leave all your money to mammy so she can buy me some decent toys", she said to my wife the other day.

> R. Void
> Northwich

★★★

TOP TIP: Suck the eyes from attacking zombies using a Black & Decker 'Dustbuster'. The zombies will then wander aimlessly and can be dispatched by the usual methods at a more leisurely pace.

> **J.T., Thropton**

★★★

'MONEY can't buy me love'. So said Lennon and McCartney in the sixties. But I can't help thinking that perhaps they could have avoided ending up hitched to a couple of boilers like Yoko and Linda if they'd spent a bit of their cash on decent haircuts, instead of both using the same pudding bowl.

> T. Robin Gristle
> Bristol

THESE so-called 'Christians' tell us that God is in all places at all times. If that's the case that means he's constantly in Paul Raymond's Revue Bar in Soho. Perhaps these Jesus freaks could explain what in the Devil's name he is doing there?

> K. Green
> London W11

LAST week council workmen built a new wall at the bottom of our road. Who said British workmen are lazy?

> Mrs C. Jefferies
> Wolverhampton

★★

TOP TIP: Agrophobics. Feel more comfortable in large open spaces by looking the right way through a pair of binoculars.

> **T. R. Ilbey, Hattington**

★★

'CATCHPHRASE' host Roy Walker is constantly telling contestants to "Say what you see". So why isn't every answer "A smug Irish git"?

> J. Taylor
> Oxford

YOU often hear women say that 'all men are the same with the lights off'. Well, perhaps some of your female readers would like to pop round to my house for a shag. My electricity was cut off last week.

> Richard Button-Mushroom
> Ripon

IT'S surely one of life's great paradoxes that having 'green fingers' means you are a good gardener, whilst having brown fingers means you can't wipe your arse properly.

> M. H.
> Bakewell

POLICE, magistrates and sober citizens all tell us that it is neither big nor clever to drink. Well I drink 15 pints a day, I'm 6 foot 3 inches tall, and a Professor of Theoretical Physics at Manchester University.

> Prof R. Hough
> Manchester

★★

TOP TIP: Claustrophobics. Reduce the risk of panic when entering a lift by looking through the wrong end of a pair of binoculars.

> **T. R. Ilbey, Hattington**

★★

THEY say that all property is theft. But they also say that *possession is nine tenths of the law*. Given that you *possess* all your property, *theft* is therefore nine tenths of the law. But try telling that to the judge next time you're up for shop lifting.

> H. Mence
> H M Prison, Dartmoor

"WAR! What is it good for?" asked Edwin Starr in his 1970 pop hit. Well Mr Starr, releasing Europe from the grip of a genocidal megalomaniac is one thing that springs to mind.

> P. Pom
> Harwich

IF the best things in life are free, how come the ten pints of lager and chicken Madras I had on Saturday night, which were fucking great, cost me twenty-four quid?

> M. Ireland
> Leamington Spa

★★

TOP TIP: Lamb for dinner tonight and you've forgotten the mint sauce? No worries. Toothpaste mixed with a little vinegar and chopped nettle leaves makes an ideal emergency replacement.

> **J.T., Thropton**

★★

'ALWAYS expect the unexpected', or so the saying goes. Correct me if I'm wrong, but if you expect something, it cannot be unexpected. 'Always expect the expected' would therefore seem a more practical piece of advice.

> T. Holmes
> Bayswater

"YOU'RE going home in a fucking ambulance", my mate and I shouted at an elderly man as he lay helpless on the ground at a football match recently. He eventually saw the funny side when he realised we were St John's Ambulance men and we were coming to take him home after he'd fallen and twisted an ankle.

> A. Robin
> London

DO-GOODERS say that we're all to blame for the increasing crime levels on our streets. Well I'm not. I was in the pub with me mates. Honest.

J. Walsh
Newbiggin

★★★

TOP TIP: Acquire the coolest garden in your street by placing Rayban sunglasses on your gnomes and replacing their fishing rods with small toy shotguns.

N. Aitchison, Nicosia, Cyprus

★★★

I READ in a magazine recently that eating too many onions can cause amnesia. This is nonsense. Alcohol is the cause of amnesia, which is why characters in films often 'drink to forget', rather than eating onions.

Ethel Bint
Crawley

SOME people say that swearing is the sign of a limited vocabulary. Well, I write dictionaries for a living and have a big vocabulary, but I still swear.
So that fucks that theory, doesn't it?

Lornal Knight, Editor
Collins English Dictionaries

WHO said cork doesn't float? The other day while I was having a bath a cork tile fell from the wall and landed in the water. It proceeded to float on the surface, entirely unaided, until I retrieved it several moments later.

Jack Wilson
Potters Bar

Stars In Your Eyes

NOT so long ago I dreamt I was lying naked in bed next to beautiful 'Woman of Substance' actress Jenny Seagrove. Imagine my surprise when I awoke the next morning to find that I was!

> Michael Winner
> (Fat, rich, pointy nosed
> film director), London

★★★

TOP TIP: Create your own bidet by simply installing a 'widget' in your toilet pan. Hey presto! A ringpiece jet wash with every flush.

> **John Tait, Thropton**

★★★

I ENJOY watching pro-celebrity golf and tennis, but how about pro-celebrity boxing? I would gladly pay £25 to watch Jonathan King slug it out for ten rounds with Frank Bruno.

> A. Anderson
> Hull

WHAT Nanette Newman fails to tell TV viewers is that with the amount of money you could save by not buying Fairy Liquid you could almost pay to eat all your meals in a restaurant. In which case you wouldn't have any bleeding dishes to wash.

> B. Jones
> Biddlecombe

MY son said he was having a 'Pop Tart' for breakfast. Imagine my surprise when I came downstairs to find him groping TV celebrity Paula Yates on the breakfast table.

Mrs B. Hearn
Droitwich

IF that Sinead O'Connor grew her hair a bit and bought herself a nice frock or two she'd make a lovely wife for some lucky young man.

Mrs E. Roach
Durham

★★

TOP TIP: Office workers. Half a ball of Edam cheese makes a handy desk top 'pen cushion', and can be nibbled if you become peckish between meals.

A. Madeupname,
Ficticiousplace

★★

IF Michael Winner was an MP he'd have no trouble complying with the Nolan Committee's recommendations concerning declaration of income. In fact you'd have to prosecute the fat sod to shut him up and stop him telling every fucker how much loot he's got, where every last penny came from, and what he's been spending it on this week. The fat, arrogant, fat, self-obsessed, draft dodging, fat bastard. And his bird's a gold-digging slag heap too. Probably.

A.Stenson
Stockport

I LOOK forward to Hollywood celebrities dying because then we get to see all their best movies on TV. I hope Clint Eastwood dies next, as I'm a huge fan of his films.

Mrs F. J. Sommaville
Norwich

IF one female news reader started reading the news with her top off everyone would tune in. Before you know it they'd all have to get them off in order to compete for viewers. Then all the weather girls would start getting them off too. I can't wait.

Jim Carter
Oulton, Norfolk

★★

TOP TIP: Give your pet tortoise protective 'bull bars' by slipping the wire off a champagne cork over his head.

J. Bobble, Tinsley

★★

GEORGE Michael has already sold over 15 million copies of his first solo album, and has made so much money that he could retire tomorrow and never work again. So why doesn't he?

Mr I. Toadflax
Chickweed, Herts.

CONGRATULATIONS to the Queen on doing such a marvellous job, taking the time and trouble to make a speech on television so soon after finishing her Christmas dinner. With the meal over and the dishes done most of us would simply sit back with our feet up for the remainder of the afternoon. But not the Queen. She deserves every penny she gets. And more.

Mrs L. Hammond
Suffolk

I FIND it quite sickening to see billions of dollars being spent on this so-called 'Hubble space telescope' when the best it can possible achieve is to send back yet more blurred and boring pictures which don't even look like space. Surely for a fraction of the cost these scientists could come up with a telescope that could see through Catherine Zeta-Jones' bedroom window. It would be far cheaper to maintain, and at last we'd have some pictures worth looking at.

> A. Peppercorn
> York

★★

TOP TIP: Try using Cola cubes instead of Oxo cubes. Not only will it put the fizz back into tired old recipes, it also considerably reduces the risk of BSE.

> **Daisy Duke, Hazzard**

★★

IN the old days of black and white television I always used to get confused between news reader Robert Dougal and Dougal the dog from the Magic Roundabout. Ironically now that I have a colour set neither are on TV very often.

> S. Ternant
> Cumbria

★★

TOP TIP: An XR3i Cabriolet with the roof down makes a perfect roller skate for dinosaurs.

> **Dale Wadman, Leics.**

★★

DELIA Smith once told TV viewers that there is nothing worse than a soggy souffle. As an AIDS sufferer I must disagree with Miss Smith's somewhat blinkered view.

> D.R.
> Kent

MY wife has gone Gladiators potty. Just the other day she came down for breakfast without touching the floor by swinging from one chandelier to another, then stood on top of the fridge and knocked me off my chair with a standard lamp. This morning she topped it all by injecting herself with steroids and growing a beard and moustache.

Reg Taylor
Bromsgrove

★★

TOP TIP: Lorry drivers. Keep your indicator on for half an hour after each manoeuvre in order to keep us car drivers on our toes.

S. Macreary, Hollingworth

★★

I HAVE an unusual hobby - playing word games with the names of pop stars. For instance 'ABBA' is a palindrome - it spells the same backwards. 'DOING JIGGY JIGGY WITH MADONNA IN A BATH FULL OF SWARFEGA' isn't a palindrome. I just like writing it down and thinking about it.

Mick Dwyer
Brighton

★★

TOP TIP: Fill a flat fish with hot butter last thing at night and it makes an ideal hot water bottle. Wake up in the morning and 'voila!' A ready cooked kipper for breakfast in bed.

Barry Clarver, Exeter

★★

TWENTY-FIVE years ago when I first met my wife she was going out with the pop singer Brian Ferry. Well, if Mr Ferry fancies taking her back now, he's more than fucking welcome to.

A.T. S.
Newcastle

I EXPLAINED to my bank manager that I was in dire straits, and he promptly offered me a loan of up to £2,000. There had been some confusion. I was of course referring to the band 'Dire Straits', of which I am the lead singer.

Mark Knoplfler
Some big house in America

HOW is it that all the lesbians in the TV soaps are good looking birds? They're about as true to life as the tuppence tugging tarts on the porno movie channel. Where's all the big booted, tattooed, shaven headed fanny eating monsters you see in real life?

Barry Marsh
Fulchester

★★★

TOP TIP: Convert any old hat to a smart 'Sherlock Holmes' style deerstalker by draping a pair of socks down over your ears before donning the hat. Remember to catch the socks when your hat is doffed.

Robert Stetson, Jedburgh

★★★

IN a recent interview Simply Red's Mick Hucknall declared he was still a socialist despite his success. Yes Mick. And you're good looking as well. That's why all those birds go out with you.

Samantha
Cheltenham

I AM a big fan of the clever Guinness TV adverts, with their challenging visual imagery, the sophisticated air of illusion, and the maturity and mystique which actor Rutger Hauer provides. If I have one criticism, it is that they fail to mention the fact Guinness turns your shit to treacle.

P. McMurphy
Derby

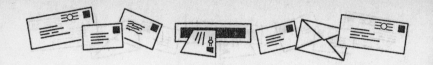

I SHARE my birthday (16th April) with 'Little Jimmy Osmond' who sang 'Long Haired Lover from Liverpool' in the early seventies. Ironically, I have fairly long hair myself, and used to live only 12 minutes away from Liverpool by train.

Simone Glover
Tottenham

★★★

TOP TIP: Polo mints make excellent 'spearmint washers' for drinking water taps, and after a drink of water they leave your breath minty fresh.

Ramindar Plinth, Ilford

★★★

IF Keith Chegwin is an example of what alcoholics can achieve by beating the booze, mine's another bottle of Pils.

R. Rogers
Dudley

★★★

TOP TIP: Collect your farts in sandwich bags during the winter. Store them in a safe place, and come the summer these handy "Pump packets" will make ideal firelighters for barbecues etc.

Andy Rogers, Fenham

★★★

I MUST admit I was never a fan of British Gas. But all that changed when I saw their brilliant TV advertisement featuring Burt Reynolds. Ever since then I've done all my cooking with gas. Of course prior to that I'd run my gas cooker with fucking Duracell batteries, hadn't I.

B. Jones
Biddlecombe

Chapter Eleven

Points of You Two

IT is a popular misconception among feminists that men look upon all women as sex objects. Sex objects? Most of them are so ugly I wouldn't shag them if you paid me.

F. Haskins
Peckham

★★

TOP TIP: Car tyres painted white and wrapped in green tarpaulin sheets make ideal packets of Polos for short sighted giants.

E.F.Gee, Aitchaye

★★

DOESN'T the Queen Mum look marvellous for her age. I am currently trying to imitate her radiant looks and lovely smile by painting my teeth yellow and sleeping with the face immersed in vinegar.

Does anyone know where I can buy a silly hat?

J. Devine
Edgware

★★

HOW often do we hear of people dying on their "deathbeds". My advice to anyone seeing one of these "deathbeds" is to stay well away and on no account get onto it. Surely it is time the Government took action and banned these contraptions altogether.

R. McRoberts (Mrs)
Belfast

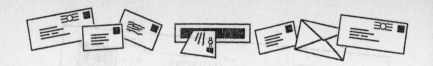

IT strikes me as something of an anomaly that health authorities are being quoted prices approaching quarter of a million pounds for X-ray machines, while X-ray spectacles can be bought for a couple of pounds by mail order. Someone, somewhere is making a healthy profit.

J. Tait
Thropton

★★

TOP TIP: Fishermen. A dead rabbit makes an ideal grow bag for maggots.

Pam Anahat, Huddersfield

★★

THE Government prints a health warning on all cigarette packets. Wouldn't a wise precaution to prevent the spread of AIDS be to print a similar warning on the bottom of all the homosexuals?

Mrs R. Burr
East Dulwich

USING lead free petrol is hardly a great sacrifice to make in order to save the planet. Some of these so-called environmentalists should try using lead free pencils.

P. Northwich
Morley

★★

TOP TIP: Traffic cops. Don't waste time and money installing video cameras in your cars. Install them in the front and rear windows of all Volvo 340s and Maestros driven by old age pensioners. That way all the accidents which the doddering old fogies cause will be recorded on tape.

Andrew Davies
Yarm, Smoggieland

★★

IF the heather that these so-called Gypsies sell is so lucky, how come, despite having bunches of it themselves, they're reduced to flogging it in the streets to earn a few bob?

G. Ivatt
Derby

★★

TOP TIP: Wear trousers back to front. That way you'll never get the 'little fella' caught in your zip.

G. Adams, Croydon

★★

IT'S all well and good for Greenpeace activists to jump about all day complaining about pollution in the sea. But the minute these hypocrites get home they go and shit in the toilet, just like everybody else. They ought to set an example to others by shitting onto a piece of newspaper, and putting it in the dustbin.

Mr S. Vesta
Chow Mein

I WONDER why English restaurants don't serve the feet when cooking rabbits. After all, the French eat frogs' legs. You never know, it may bring good luck to those who dared eat them.

P. A. Walton
Chesterfield

★★★

TOP TIP: Dog owners. Give passers-by the impression that your dog is well trained by ordering it to do whatever it happens to be doing already.

J. Kay, Elem, N.P.

★★★

WHY don't they play the tennis final on the first day of the Wimbledon fortnight instead of waiting till the end when the courts are all worn and bumpy? It's ridiculous expecting top class players to perform on less than perfect playing surfaces.

Laurie Penfold
Sheffield

★★★

TOP TIP: Motorists. Enjoy the freedom of cycling by removing your windscreen, sticking half a melon skin on your head, then jumping red lights and driving the wrong way up one way streets.

Maurice Traveller, Brentford

★★★

CUSTOMS and Excise tell us that for every pound of drugs they seize ten times that amount gets through. Well if they want fewer drugs getting through why don't they seize a smaller amount? Ideally they should seize none at all, since ten times nothing is nothing.

C. Pasty
Padstowe

I'M sick and tired of the Royal knockers. Why oh why won't these people give Fergie a chance, instead of criticising her the minute she pisses off to the south of France with some dodgy Texan slap head and all our loot.

N. Quazar
Godalming

★★

TOP TIP: X File fans. Create the effect of being abducted by aliens by drinking two bottles of vodka. You'll invariably wake up in a strange place the following morning, having had your memory mysteriously 'erased'.

Sam Neffendorf, Weybridge

★★

RATHER than going through the trauma of a public divorce, why doesn't the Prince of Wales stick with tradition and have his wife beheaded? This would solve at a stroke any disputes as to whether or not Diana should become Queen, or retain the style 'HRH'.

Neil Wood
Blackburn

★★

TOP TIP: High blood pressure sufferers. Simply cut yourself and bleed for while, thus reducing the pressure in your veins.

N. Rodwell, Herne Bay, Kent

★★

MRS THATCHER tells us that capital punishment should be returned. It's all well and good punishing people in London, but what about the provinces? Cities like Manchester, Leeds and Newcastle? Surely the reintroduction of capital punishment would only serve to widen the 'North-South divide'.

F. Grunblatt
Sunderland

APPARENTLY the long hours of darkness are to blame for the appallingly high suicide rate in Scandinavia during the winter. Perhaps if the Scandinavians tried using a higher wattage of lamp bulb to brighten up their lives, instead of drinking gallons of vodka and watching animal pornography all night long, they might not feel so readily disposed towards topping themselves.

>   Vincent Wulff
>   Kinross

★★

TOP TIP: Gents. After visiting the barber remove hairs from the back of your neck by inflating a balloon, rubbing it on your jumper in order to charge it with static electricity, and then gently brushing it along the collar line and around your ears.

>   **B. Derby-Hatt, Luton**

★★

I REMEMBER the Coronation in 1953. We kids had a marvellous time at our street party. Wouldn't it be nice if the Queen popped her clogs soon, then we could have another one.

>   J. Askey
>   Bournemouth

★★

TOP TIP: Gentlemen. Never smoke a cigar larger than your penis as this may invite witticisms from former partners.

>   **John Butler, Liverpool L17**

★★

MONEY talks, or so they say. Surely with today's technology this could become a reality. Imagine the advantages for blind people if battery operated coins were designed to speak their value when taken out of your pocket.

>   T. McDermott
>   Bury

WOULDN'T it be a good idea for all the countries in the world to sit down and sort out the sides for the next world war, rather than leaving it till the last minute as in the past? This time I think Japan should be on our side for a change, and Germany can have America 'cos the yanks tend to kill quite a few of our soldiers no matter which side they're on. We can toss a coin for who gets the Italians.

P. Lancer
Rochester

★★

TOP TIP: When standing on a chair to change a light bulb always put the chair in position, below the light, before standing on it. It becomes much harder to move the chair once you are standing on it.

T. Macroadstone, Derby

★★

PEOPLE who take drugs should be locked up. The other day a policeman took all my drugs, and I'd just paid sixty quid for them.

Madd
Braintree

HAVING closed circuit TV surveillance in our shops and in our streets to cut crime is all well and good. But how do we know that the people monitoring the TV screens are behaving themselves? How do we know they aren't constantly zooming in on the bottoms and bouncing breasts of sexually attractive young ladies as they innocently walk down the High Street? If they've got nothing to hide then they won't mind if we have closed circuit cameras monitoring their control rooms, keeping an eye out for any suspicious hand-in-pocket rhythmic shenanigans going on in the trouser department.

Phillippa Legg
Lyndhurst

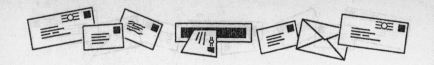

★★★

TOP TIP: Before attempting to remove stubborn stains from a garment always circle the stain in permanent marker pen so that when you remove the garment from your washing machine you can easily find where the stain was a..d check to make sure it has gone.

Miss Elizabeth Williams, Solihull

★★★

WHAT a talented bunch the Royal Family are. Of the six immediate members no less than three have represented their country at various sports. Prince Charles plays polo, Princess Anne is an accomplished show jumper, and the Duke of Edinburgh a coach and horses driver. And if drinking gin or choking on fish bones ever become Olympic sports I dare say there's another couple of gold medals in it for us.

Mr F. Prunes
Syrup

★★★

TOP TIP: Townies. Whenever you see country folk driving into town in their green Range Rovers to go shopping, jump up and down screaming "Get off my land!" Then shoot their dog.

Y. Pages, Cheshire

★★★

THERE has been a lot of TV coverage recently devoted to the subject of transvestites. I can't help feeling there are enough ugly women in this world already without men having to dress up as them.

Jim McAteer
London, SE15

Chapter Twelve

And Finally Cyril ...

I DON'T see why dog owners should be fined if their dog fouls the pavement. If a dog owner was caught drink/driving, they wouldn't expect his dog to pay the fine. This is clearly a case of double standards.

> Mrs D. Kent
> Wimbledon

IF drugs are such a problem on the streets of Britain why was I arrested at Heathrow airport for trying to smuggle cannabis on a plane to America? Surely I should be congratulated for attempting to take this substance out of the country.

> Mr S. Rule
> H M Prison, Hull

★★

TOP TIP: Make rowing a boat easier by drilling a few large holes through the oars.

> **John Tait, Thropton**

★★

INSTEAD of buying Lottery tickets every week I purchase a tin of beans and plant them in the ground. For the price of one Lottery ticket I can buy over 1000 beans. And let's face it, there's a far better chance one of my beans will grow into a giant beanstalk and lead me up to a magical kingdom in the clouds full of treasure, than there is of me ever winning the Lottery.

> P. Rhodes
> Glossop

WHO needs a £40 million win on the lottery to find happiness? Up my way £20 will buy seven pints of lager, a kebab and chips and a hand job in the Co-op doorway. I'm a winner every Saturday night!

Bristler Bain
Manchester

★★

TOP TIP: Heavy smokers. Don't throw away those filters from the end of your cigarettes. Save them up and within a few years you'll have enough to insulate your loft.

Mr J. Hedley, Northumberland

★★

I WAS hoping you could help me by printing the following message for my husband who popped out for a pint of milk two years ago and hasn't returned.
"Barry. If there's no silver top, semi-skimmed will do".

Mrs Olivia Britton
Didbury, Manchester

★★

TOP TIP: Make 'thick' stamps costing only two pence by filing a 2p piece into a rectangular shape and painting it red.

R. Yarwood, Runcorn

★★

I ALMOST ran into the back of a slow moving hearse on a main road recently. As the law requires tractors and other slow moving vehicles to display a flashing amber light, would it not be a good idea for hearses to display similar flashing lights? And perhaps as an extra safety feature they could play a loud, catchy tune, like an ice cream van.

A. Rayleigh
Sidcup

ON Saturday nights it seems I just can't drink enough beer, because every Sunday morning I'm still thirsty.

E. B. Cushion
Worcester

IF Samantha Fox could sing half as well as she can grow tits she'd be number one in the charts all year round.

M. Henderson
Whitley Bay

★★★

TOP TIP: Action men embedded in a half a grapefruit make 'extra large' Subbuteo footballers suitable for adults.

I.C., Grimsby

★★★

AS a society we ask the brave men and women of the police to put themselves at risk every day in order to protect us from crime. Yet we, as a society, then complain the minute they beat a few black people up, forge the odd statement, or jail a few innocent paddies. Let's give Britain's bobbies our backing for a change. They deserve it.

Det. Con. D. Witherspoon
West Midlands CID

I WAS really worried the other day when I saw a ticket inspector getting on the train - I didn't have a ticket. Then suddenly I remembered, I didn't need one. I was the driver.

D. Woods
Romford

★★★

TOP TIP: Internet users. Save yourself a lot of time and money by simply ringing a public call box and waiting for some sad bastard to walk by with nothing better to do than answer it.

S. Hope, Long Eaton

★★★

AFTER having sex with my next door neighbour's wife I fell asleep with my head under the pillow. I awoke in a pool of blood with most of my teeth missing.
I like to think that the fairies took them. Do any other readers have similar unusual or quirky superstitions?

L. Redshaw
Boston

★★

TOP TIP: Wheelchair basketball coaches. Miss out Lourdes from any forthcoming European tours in order to avoid losing your star players.

G. Hogg, Lanarkshire

★★★

I JUST had to tell your readers about the most sensational blow job I got the other day off a middle aged bird who was wearing a pin striped skirt and jacket. She runs an entertainments agency and got me a six month contract playing trumpet on board the QE2.

B. Balderstone
Peterlee

I THOUGHT my luck was in the day a pretty girl approached me in the pub and asked if I could get her a drink. Then I remembered - I was serving behind the bar at the time.

Tony Noble
Burnley

★★

TOP TIP: A sheet of sand paper makes a cheap and effective substitute for costly maps when visiting the Sahara desert.

A. T. Loveday, Ramsgate, Kent

★★

I WAS dreading the boss arriving at work last week as I'd heard he was going to give me a carpeting. Then I remembered; I'm the boardroom. And not only was I being carpeted, I was also getting new curtains.

A. Boardroom
Preston

★★

TOP TIP: Convince neighbours that you have invented a 'shrinking' device by ruffling your hair, wearing a white laboratory coat, and parking a JCB digger outside your house for a few days. Then dim and flicker the lights in your house during the night and replace the JCB, unseen, with a Tonka toy of the same description. Watch their faces the next morning!

Prof. J. Francis, Rhondda

★★

I DREAD the changing of the clocks each year because it means that for three weeks, until I get used to it, I get my morning stiffy while I'm waiting at the bus stop.

Mark Carnforth
Brighton

IF Linda McCartney would stop trying to sing, do hand claps and play mini-moog on Paul's records, I will become a vegetarian and so will three of my mates. So come on Linda. Which is more important? Pretending to be a pop star, or the lives of countless innocent farm animals?

P Abbot
Newent

THIS Government are all in favour of a return to Victorian values. Well if any Tory MP in the cabinet wants to sell me their house, I'll give them five hundred pounds ten shillings and sixpence for it.

W. I. Finial
Putney

★★★

TOP TIP: Glue CD's together back-to-back. Play one side, then flip it over and play the other. Just like your old vinyl records.

Warren Wilson
Chifley, Australia

★★★

I'M fed up with moaning minnies who complain about all the repeats on TV. If they don't like them, why didn't they complain about them the first time they were on?

Alan Wingnut
Halfinch Dowel

SIR Andrew-Lloyd Webber has just bought a Canaletto from Sotherbys for ten million quid. Well I've just bought a can of lager from Tescos for 39p. Who's the cunt?

E. O'Dross
Reigate

*Viz magazine is published every two months.
You can buy it in shops, or write to it
at the following address:*

LetterBocks
Viz Commick
P.O. Box 1 PT
Newcasle upon Tyne
NE99 1PT

LetterB·cKs

It's hip, it's hop, it's all the rage
It's Britain's crappest letters page

If you're wrong or if you're right
Take your trousers off and shite

**Fucking wanky bell-end tit
Hairy arseholes bollocks clit**

The End